EssaySnark's Strategies for the
2014-'15 MBA Admissions Essays for
COLUMBIA BUSINESS SCHOOL

EssaySnark's Strategies for the 2014-'15 MBA Admissions Essays for COLUMBIA BUSINESS SCHOOL

by EssaySnark®

Snarkolicious Press

Paperback edition May 15, 2014
version 4.0

Snarkolicious Press
PO Box 50021
Palo Alto, CA 94303

www.snarkoliciouspress.com

978 1 938098 19 2

© 2011-2014 by EssaySnark®

Cover image © Eric Isselée, used under license from Fotolia.com

All rights reserved.

No part of this book may be reproduced or transmitted in any form or by any means, electronic or mechanical, including photocopying, recording, or by an information storage system, without permission from the publisher.

This publication is provided "as is", without warranty of any kind, either express or implied. The author and Snarkolicious Press assume no liability for errors or omissions in this publication or other documents which are referenced or linked to this publication. While we certainly hope that you will be successful in your quest for admission to an MBA program, we cannot offer any promises that you will be, whether or not you adopt the advice provided herein. In no event shall Snarkolicious Press or its authors, principals, subsidiaries, partners, or owners, be liable for any special, incidental, indirect or consequential damages of any kind, or any damages whatsoever, arising out of or in conjunction with the use or performance of this information. Applicants to any graduate program or university should verify the school's policies, application requirements, processes, procedures, and other criteria. This publication could include technical or other inaccuracies or typographical errors. Changes are periodically added to the information herein; these changes will be incorporated into new editions of this publication. Thus, different versions or formats of this publication may include different information.

Look for other *SnarkStrategies Guides* (digital and paperback) at your favorite bookseller or on the EssaySnark blahg at http://essaysnark.com.

Follow EssaySnark on Twitter!

"Risk comes from not knowing what you're doing."

Warren Buffett

About this *SnarkStrategies Guide*

This *SnarkStrategies Guide* covers the most important elements of the MBA admissions process at Columbia Business School, including a complete discussion of the 2014 essay questions and all the essential information you need to understand rolling admissions, Early Decision, and the J-Term. Columbia does admissions differently from other business schools, and we cover everything you need to know if you are interested in applying to this powerhouse school.

To set expectations right here at the front: **EssaySnark will not tell you what to write in your essays.** Sorry. We will tell you about some silly things that we've seen countless others do in their Columbia applications, so that you can hopefully avoid such missteps. And, we'll demystify the unique landscape that is the Columbia admissions process, so that you're an educated consumer coming in. Plenty of Brave Supplicants do just fine in hunkering down with these tips and their own first-hand research and applying on their own.

As with any school, you will gain a lot by visiting campus, sitting in on a class, and interacting with current students. This type of on-the-ground research can be incredibly helpful in understanding what the school is about and what they're looking for in their students.

Of course, if you still find yourself stuck, drop on over to our blahg at http://essaysnark.com or email us at gethelpnow@essaysnark.com and we'll see what we can do to help out.

Table of Contents

Some recent Columbia history..1
    Another reason to do your Columbia research early..2
What Columbia Looks For..3
Your Columbia Application Strategy:
You Need to Know What You Want to Do..5
    Why you should apply early: Rolling Admissions..5
    EssaySnark's Inexact Guidelines for When to Apply..10
    How much of an advantage is Early Decision?...11
Columbia's Short-Answer Question: Short-Term Goal...14
    So what's a bad career goal?..20
Columbia's Essay 1: Why MBA (Which Is Really: Goals)...24
    What needs to go in Essay 1?..24
Essay 2: Columbia at the Center...29
    What needs to go in Essay 2?..30
Columbia's Essay 3: Who Are You?...32
    What needs to go in Essay 3?..32
Optional Essay..35
Reapplicant Essay...36
What to Do Next...37

Some recent Columbia history

Before we go into the details of how to apply to Columbia, we need to make mention of where Columbia is at in terms of its reputation and ranking. You may have noticed that BusinessWeek pushed Columbia down to #14 in its 2012 rankings list – from #9. That is a significant drop. As in, SIGNIFICANT. Not just because it's 5 points, but because it pushes Columbia out of the esteemed Top 10. Perhaps you're reading this in the middle of the admissions season, when new BusinessWeek rankings have been released, and, we're guessing, Columbia has recovered its standing somewhat. However, as of this writing (May 2014) Columbia is still in that down-and-out position.

There are many factors that go into the BusinessWeek ranking and we're not going to dig into all of them here, and there were many contributors to this drop in placement in 2012. The *BusinessWeek* rankings come out every other November (they're a biannual list) and in 2012, they incorporated trends in application volumes at all the schools for the 2011-'12 admissions cycle. Those were candidates who applied for the Class of 2014. In that application year, Columbia experienced a massive hit in applications – down 19%.

Why?

EssaySnark went through a full series of posts on this topic on the blahg which you're invited to read: http://essaysnark.com/2012/09/columbia-no-longer-a-favorite/

Our hypothesis is that the very unflattering portrayal of Columbia's Dean Hubbard and a Columbia professor in the 2010 movie *Inside Job* had an effect on people thinking about going to business school. Since you're considering an application to Columbia Business School, we recommend you check this movie out.

Some things reported in the film have changed in the last five years, but only marginally. That professor is still there – though they have a new policy on disclosure of outside compensation, so he now posts a list on his website of who's paying him for consulting. Dean Hubbard is still running the show.

Maybe the filmmakers got it wrong. There's a lot of factors that contributed to the economic collapse of 2008. And maybe EssaySnark's getting it wrong, in terms of the cause of Columbia's drop in applications in 2011. No matter how you feel about the dean and that professor, there's plenty to like about Columbia.

You simply need to be an educated consumer.

By starting off with this dose of buzzkill, it may seem that we're totally down on this school, but we're not. We've seen some real changes there, particularly in how they're running admissions now. Following the 2011 season debacle, Columbia made some, ah, *adjustments* in its admissions staff, and in the past few years, we're seeing them work for the attention and respect of the community of business school applicants. There's much less of a sense of entitlement coming from the place than we previously perceived. We're feeling kinda fond of Columbia again.

However, our opinion really doesn't matter, and so we begin this *Guide* with the same advice we give to everyone, applying to all schools: Go out and do some research.

In the case of Columbia, the most important part of the task is talk to people. Reach out to current students. Connect with some alumni. Work your network and see who you know who went to Columbia – and also, who you know who went elsewhere, and why. Especially important: Talk to recruiters in your target field and see what their impressions of the place are. Do some informational interviews with hiring managers in your industry and hear what they think.

Most of the Columbia grads we've ever encountered are good people, motivated, accomplished, sincere. We're not trying to paint the entire school community with this tainted brush. We do, however, feel an obligation to educate you on an aspect of Columbia Business School that you may care about. As with all things, the only opinion that matters is your own. And despite an appearance to the contrary, we happen to like Columbia Business School. We have plenty of former clients walking the halls there. We hope they do better in BusinessWeek's 2014 rankings, and we wish everyone graduating now and in the future great success. Maybe you'll be one of them in 2017?

Another reason to do your Columbia research early

There's so many reasons for doing this research on a school – and with Columbia, you actually need to research them, and research the other schools you're interested in, too. If you think you like Columbia best, but you haven't based this opinion on any hard data like visiting the schools, then we strongly encourage you to get yourself on campus at at least some of those other schools before deciding to do a Columbia Early Decision application.

If you're applying to Columbia J-Term or through the Regular Decision round, then this is not as important. However, as we will fully discuss in this *Guide*, the Columbia Early Decision application is *binding*. That means, if you apply there, you're saying in advance that that's where you'll go if they accept you. That's great, it's a real advantage to you the applicant in terms of how they'll consider your app – they like people that like them – but the issue is, you need to be absolutely certain that Columbia is indeed your first choice school.

We have seen more than one BSer apply to Columbia in Early Decision, and only after that app was submitted did they go to visit other schools – and then they regretted their Columbia hastiness. In some cases, Columbia said "no" and they came out successful at those other schools later – but with at least one such dude, he got into Columbia, and so that's where he went. He ended up very happy with the decision – Columbia was, in fact, a great choice for him – but he went through some consternation along the way.

This *Guide* explains all about the nooks and crannies of the very unique Columbia processes so read on to learn all that you need to develop your strategy – for Columbia by itself, and in conjunction with the other schools that will make up your application strategy.

What Columbia Looks For

Let's start with a list of what Columbia cares about most in evaluating candidates for admissions.

NOTE: THERE ARE ALWAYS EXCEPTIONS. These are just the rough generalities for trends and preferences in the admissions process that we've seen at Columbia Business School over many years now. Columbia has been quite consistent for some time in their choosing **more experienced** candidates, and in favoring applicants who have **clear and reasonable career goals**.

The critical elements of a successful profile for Columbia tend to be:

> **1. Work Experience.** Columbia prefers somewhat older candidates. Even superstars coming straight out of college who may have an easy time getting into another good school will likely have trouble at Columbia. If you're still in school or just graduated, this is probably not the best place to try right now.
>
> - *What's a "minimum" number of years of work experience?* Two, though three is better. If you graduated from college in 2012, you could try applying to Columbia this year, but you'd be better off waiting a year – unless you're out-and-out amazing, in which case they'll find a spot for you.
>
> - *Is there a maximum?* Not really, but most Columbia F/T MBA students are in their 20s, with a number are in their 30s, and there's someone in his 40s every now and then. They actively redirect much-older candidates to the EMBA program when those applicants are local to Manhattan (we have a post on the blahg about this; see the Columbia Essay Questions page for a list of the important ones).
>
> **2. Career, both past and future.** Columbia is a finance school, and yet they offer a lot of other very strong "areas of focus" (as they call them), including marketing, real estate and entrepreneurship, among others. They obviously send a lot of graduates to Wall Street and to the major consulting firms. Columbia is friendly to candidates from a variety of backgrounds, as long as they're not *too* different. If you're an opera singer by training, you'll need to do a bang-up job in showing why you now need an MBA. The career goals and how they are expressed matter a LOT at Columbia; in fact, it's what most of this *Guide* is about. The main point to keep in mind? Columbia is most definitely not "just" a finance school.
>
> **3. GMAT.** Because of their larger class size, Columbia has the luxury of being able to admit students from a broader range of profiles without adversely affecting their averages too much. So, you do not necessarily need to be above the 700 mark on your GMAT to get into Columbia. At the same time, if you're going into finance (or if you've been in finance) and you don't score well on the quant side of the GMAT, you may have a tougher time of it during the Columbia admissions process, since obviously you're going to need those skills in your career. If you have a lower GMAT then you should seriously consider applying through the Early Decision process – provided that Columbia is your #1 choice. More on ED later.

4. GPA. Columbia has traditionally given less leeway to applicants who have rocky academics. Anything below a 3.0 GPA equivalent (on the U.S. 4.0 scale) will be a challenge to get into the F/T tracks; the EMBA has a little looser standards. If your GMAT and your GPA are both below the school's averages, you're going to have to work hard to compensate for these in other areas and to be honest, this can be an uphill battle at a school like Columbia. We discuss both low GPA and low GMAT in many topics on our blahg at http://essaysnark.com.

Conversely, many applicants with high GPAs – above 3.5 or 3.6 – *especially with an Early Decision application,* discover that it's fairly easy to get an offer from Columbia.

5. Hireability. All things considered, the net-net assessment that the Columbia adcom is doing of your entire profile is focused on ***hireability***. They want to be convinced that you'll be able to get a job when you graduate from their program. The bulk of this *SnarkStrategies Guide* is centered on how best to express this to your Columbia adcom reader.

Again, these are broad-strokes guidelines, not set-in-stone rules for what Columbia wants and how they'll react to a given profile. Everyone's got some weaknesses. Your job is to show Columbia how those weaknesses are not showstoppers, based on all your other great strengths.

Your Columbia Application Strategy: You Need to Know What You Want to Do

As Columbia's essay questions should make abundantly clear, and as we already alluded to with the "hireability" bullet above: **Career goals are critical at Columbia.**

Most bschools ask a "career goals" question in their admissions essays. And that makes sense, given that the MBA is supposed to be preparation for you to embark on a new career. Or at least a new-and-improved version of your existing one.

Columbia takes this as fundamental to their application evaluation process. They have for years been ultra-focused on the career goals a candidate expresses in determining whether to accept or deny that person. This year (2014), they have again underscored that theme with the questions, and particularly with the limitations on those questions. They want to hear about your plans for the future. And they want the direct version of it.

EssaySnark has always appreciated the Columbia essays for how much they focus the candidate. Going through the exercises in this *Guide* will prepare you very precisely for answering these questions – and they will also prepare you for other schools' applications, too.

That leads us to Snarky Strategy #1

> If you're applying to multiple schools, and Columbia is on that list, *do your Columbia application first.*

This is because there's a lot of heavy lifting that goes into writing your first application. You'll have a learning curve to conquer. The focus and specificity required in putting together a good set of Columbia essays will *serve you well* in most other applications, too. The effort you put in here will likely pay off in spades in helping you develop a quality presentation for those other apps later.

The obvious other reason to do Columbia's application first: **Columbia's rolling admissions.**

Why you should apply early: Rolling Admissions

Columbia handles many aspects of their admissions process differently than other schools do, with **rolling admissions** being the most important.

All application processes and rounds at Columbia are rolling.

This includes the Early Decision option for the August Start, the J-Term, and the various flavors of EMBA. All applications are processed – generally – in the order received.

Columbia opens their full-time application quite early in the season, too, which means they start looking at candidates as soon as May. They're often the first school with questions out (sometimes

HBS beats them by a few days but not this year). If you apply super early to Columbia, they will render their decision correspondingly early, too – with some exceptions, as covered below.

The other main difference is that Columbia's process is incredibly confusing. No other school's admissions is anywhere near as convoluted. We'll explain everything for Columbia's process so you understand how it works.

First note: As we've already alluded to in the list of qualities Columbia cares about on page 3: **Early Decision is a serious benefit for many people. Here's a post about Early** Decision on our blahg:

http://essaysnark.com/2010/07/round-strategies-whats-this-early-action-nonsense/

(All these important posts that we are referencing are listed on the Columbia Essay Questions page of the site.)

We'll come back to that. Keep it in the back of your mind: **Early Decision is a real advantage.**

Early Decision is not available for the J-Term. It's available for August start for full-time, and for the EMBA options.

Regardless of whether you're going for the J-Term, or August start — and regardless of whether you apply through the Regular or the Early Decision options for the August start — and even regardless of whether you're applying to the standard full-time MBA or one of the different EMBA tracks — *you should get your application in as soon as possible* – **with some caveats**. This is because of Columbia's rolling admissions. There is a huge advantage to applying earlier in the cycle for whichever program/application option you're targeting – and it will be a huge *disadvantage* if you apply too late.

The only MBA admissions at Columbia *without* rolling admissions is for the JD/MBA joint degree. Everyone else? You'll be subject to rolling admissions. This means you want to get that app in early.

Let's make it official. Snarky Strategy #2 is:

If you're applying to Columbia, for any program or any term or any application option, APPLY EARLY.

Why?

Because Columbia admissions operates on a FIFO model. FIFO is "first in, first out." (Just wait. If you don't know what that is, you'll learn all about FIFO in your accounting class in bschool.) They process applications (generally) in the order received.

Now this does NOT mean that if you apply through the Early Decision process on, say, July 1st, and your best friend applies on August 1st, that you are guaranteed to hear back from them before he does. What it does mean is that if you apply on July 1st and your candidacy is good, they're going to try to find you a spot — but if you apply in Regular Decision on, say, February 1st... they simply won't have that many spots available.

This is especially true with the J-Term, which has fewer seats available, and a much shorter admissions cycle. There can be a big difference in outcomes for someone who applies to the J-Term in July, versus the same application coming in near the deadline in October — and definitely there's a difference in how quickly you'll get a decision back. Columbia has a much lighter app volume in the summertime, and it's easier for them to get through your application more quickly than come fall, when they're under the crush of applications.

We mentioned that there are some caveats to this. Here they are:

A Snarky Caveat

Do not rush things!

You should not apply early just to be the first one in! A shabby, sloppy, or weak application makes the adcom's decision process very easy: They will not admit someone who doesn't have their act together. A mediocre application submitted early never trumps a good application submitted later – the mediocre app will never get accepted, regardless of when it's submitted. A good app has a better chance when it's submitted earlier. Most important: **Don't apply before you're truly ready!** Do not rush things just so that you get it in sooner. Work hard to make it the best app you can – but do this work as quick as you can.

> Shameless plug: The EssaySnark Complete Essay Package is a great way to move through all the steps required to build out a strong set of Columbia essays, quickly and efficiently.

There's another consideration to keep in mind: If you apply too early for either of the October deadlines, and your pitch has some good parts but not-so-good parts, there's a much greater risk of being placed on the waitlist (for the J-Term) or being offered deferred decision. Both of these are lousy outcomes.

A Snarky Caveat

You may not want to apply too early.

What is "too early", you ask?

- "Too early" means when the admissions season is still so young that Columbia has only received a smattering of applications.
- "Too early" means that there are only a few Brave Supplicants who've gone before.
- "Too early" means that the adcom doesn't yet have a good sense for how the applicant pool is shaping up.
- "Too early" means that if they like you, but they have some concerns about you, that they might put you on the waitlist instead of admitting you.

Columbia uses a waitlist for the J-Term round only. It's a holding tank for applicants they sort of like, but who they can't commit to just yet. There's a different procedure for Early Decision candidates who they sort of like but sort of don't, called "deferred decision", where they put you in an even worse limbo than this. If a J-Term application comes in and they just cannot decide, then you'll get the option of being on the waitlist, which can stay open all the way through December – yes, December! When you're supposed to be headed to class in January! It's excruciating.

There's a much greater chance you'll be placed on the waitlist if your J-Term application comes in too early, since they just won't have enough other people to compare you to. The bschool admission process is a lot about comparing you to all the other people who have also applied. The only possible advantage to submitting for the J-Term really early is that you will find out you're going on the waitlist really fast. ☺

Being offered Deferred Decision on an ED app means they ask if you want to have your app on hold until they go through the Regular Decision applicants and then they'll decide. It's basically a "No, but maybe we'll change our mind if nobody better comes along." We talk about the Deferred Decision outcome on the EssaySnark blahg:

http://essaysnark.com/2010/10/columbias-new-early-decision-process-is-lame/

Should you end up in this position, we also go into Deferred Decision a bit in the *EssaySnark Waitlist Guide*, available in our Bookstore:

http://essaysnark.com/bookstore/

Again, this caveat of "don't apply too early" pertains only to the October deadlines. There's no such thing as "too early" for the Regular Decision process in terms of advantage for your application. You can apply to RD as early as you want – though honestly, you're not going to be at a massively greater advantage for Regular Decision if you apply in June, versus October. There just won't be that many apps collecting in the queue for Regular Decision in those months in between. The adcom will also be quite well educated on what type of candidates they'll be seeing this year by the time they look at the first Regular Decision candidates, so that's why it doesn't hurt you to be a middling candidate at the top of that queue, as it could in the ED round. By the time the adcom opens the very first Regular Decision app, they already have a very good sense of how their candidate pool for the incoming class is shaping up, based on the apps received in Early Decision.

The only risk in submitting a Regular Decision application super early – like, anytime before November 1st – is that you'll have to endure the grueling process of waiting to hear back for an even more extended period of time. If you're applying Regular Decision, aim for submitting sometime in November and you're good.

EssaySnark's Inexact Guidelines for When to Apply

These are very rough guidelines for the two different full-time MBA programs – not for EMBA.

It is very possible to have a happy outcome by submitting outside these guidelines. But in an ideal world, you might try to comply.

- For the J-Term, we recommend applying **by late summer**.

- For the August start, we recommend:

    a) Apply Early Decision if you're truly serious about Columbia, in which case, submit by late summer if possible.

    b) Submit by early November if you're applying in Regular Decision and you're overeager.

    c) Submit sometime in December if you need the extra time.

    d) No matter what, submit by the Fellowship deadline in early January at the latest to have a real shot at Regular Decision. The further out into 2015 you apply, the lower your chances of getting in.

Years ago, Regular Decision apps started getting opened and invited to interview in late December. In 2013, Columbia shocked us by opening the Regular Decision round in mid-November. That schedule is likely to hold again for this 2014 season.

Even with this move-up with the processing of Regular Decision apps, submitting in December is still fine; early January is still completely viable. The November guideline we offered above is a nice-to-have but not mandatory. Really. Take the time you need to get your application right. December is a great time to submit Regular Decision – it's not so early that you're going stir-crazy for months, wondering when you'll hear back, but it's early enough to be an advantage.

Remember, the official final deadline for the Regular Decision process is in April. November or even December is plenty early, when you have that far-off date in mind.

The other big benefit with a December Columbia Regular Decision target that it's in a lull spot of the admissions cycle – well past the Round 1 craziness, with Round 2 insanity barely peeking over the corner. You will have some breathing room to focus exclusively on the Columbia essays if you decide to apply then. And, you can use your Columbia Regular Decision app to prime the pump for all the other Round 2 apps to come.

The one rule we can offer for Regular Decision: **You should not wait till the January fellowship deadline to submit.** The adcom gets the vast majority of all their applications – counting from ED, RD and J-Term combined – in the first week of January. With rolling admissions, you want to get in ahead of that crush of candidates. So apply earlier than the Fellowship deadline.

One last warning – which, with all this, should be obvious, but we'll spell it out anyway: By no means should you delay a Columbia application until February or later! We very rarely see anyone get an offer for the Columbia full-time MBA if they submit after January. It happens, it's just not typical.

So the most important part of all these complicated rules: APPLY EARLY.

But not *too early*.

How much of an advantage is Early Decision?

The Columbia adcom has said in the past that a Regular Decision application that is received early enough has just as much chance of admission as an Early Decision application. Our experience with Columbia applicants over the years does not match that. In fact, we sorta claim "bullshit" on that statement.

In the hundreds of Columbia applications we've watched through the process over the years, we definitely have noted **a very distinct advantage** in applying through Early Decision – provided that Columbia is indeed your top-choice school.

We can't say this strongly enough: PLEASE DO NOT APPLY TO EARLY DECISION JUST TO GET THE ADVANTAGE.

If you aren't committed to Columbia and you'd drop their ED offer in favor of another school, then it's simply unethical to apply in Early Decision. You are signing a commitment when you apply in ED and we really don't dig it when people are so quick to break a promise. If you have weaknesses in your profile and you're nervous about your chances, then work to improve them.

If you're not convinced ahead of time that Columbia will be your #1 choice, then you're not right for Early Decision, and that's fine. There's still plenty of spots open for Regular Decision candidates.

The timing of how and when your Columbia application is processed is near-meaningless

Once you click that little Submit button, you will drive yourself crazy with the waiting, whether you breeze straight through the process or not. The timing of when you're "supposed" to hear back, and if you "should have" received an interview invitation by now, can be a torment. The bschool discussion boards are full of this nonsense, of people posting questions about what other people's admissions process has been. Don't get caught up in all that. Just get the very best application together that you can, as early as you can, and then go distract yourself with other things (like tackling the next application). Don't fret over this part.

Of course, nobody does that. So to put your anxieties to rest as best we can, here's a rough breakout for you on this:

- Getting invited to interview relatively soon after they start reviewing apps is a good sign. It might mean you have a slightly better chance -- mostly because there are more slots still available early in the process.

- Any other change in status on your application is near-meaningless. You cannot interpret anything about your app based on how quickly or slowly it moves through all the other stages of the review cycle.

- The only exception? The timing of when your interviewer submits her report after your interview. If your status in your online application does not update for two weeks after your interview, contact the admissions office to ask them to investigate, since something went screwy (or your interviewer was asleep at the wheel).

The most important point in all this is that you need to **apply early.** (Have we mentioned that before?) So now you know you have to hustle.

Plan out your work product

Here's another important idea to consider as you are in the planning-out phase:

Snarky Strategy #3

Write your essays first.

Then **hit up your recommenders to do their thing.**

Why not get your recommenders on board first? After all, that part is easy. You could totally get them started, and feel like you're making progress on your application, when really all you're doing is procrastinating on writing the darn essays.

What EssaySnark suggests is, **get through at least the first couple drafts of your essays before**

talking to your boss about writing a recommendation. The reason for this? *Then you'll know where the holes are in your profile, and you can suggest ideas for what your boss can write about that can fill those holes.* Remember, the adcom is going to look at your application as a whole. All the pieces should work together. Not only is it important that every element of your app reinforce the others, but leveraging the recommendations in this way can also be a critical strategic opportunity for you. It's certainly one that many people overlook.

Say you get all the way through your essays, and you realize that you haven't been able to tell any teamwork stories. Well, maybe that would be a good thing for your recommenders to discuss. Or, as you're developing your material, you have to make a choice between which topics to cover in one of your essays, either using one about a project you did at work last year, or this other one about this volunteer thing you led. If you're writing your essays BEFORE your recommenders have written their letters about you, you have a lot more control. You could, for example, then decide to use the volunteer thing in your essays, and ask your boss to talk about the project from work. That way, the adcom gets both sides of you presented. If you've already had the "what should I write about" discussion with your boss, then it may be tough to go back and ask her to redirect her efforts (especially if she's already submitted it).

This is an often overlooked strategy that can really help the school see the big picture, and it can give you a little more control over how you're presenting. (Note, too, that such "what should I write about" conversations with your recommenders are perfectly fine, as long as you don't actually write their recommendations yourself!!)

So the takeaway message here: Write the essays FIRST. Then go talk to your recommenders about what they might be able to say about you.

OK. We know what you're thinking. "EssaySnark, this is a lot of build-up. I thought you were going to tell me how to tackle these darn Columbia essays?"

Yes indeed Brave Supplicant. We are now going to turn all our attention to that very important topic: *The new Columbia essay questions.*

As we already stated, the CAREER GOALS are CRITICAL for how you present to Columbia. They want to know what you want to do after you graduate with your MBA, and they want to know the SPECIFICS. Thus, we truly LOVE the new short-answer question that they're leading everything off with. This is a GREAT place to start your strategizing for your entire MBA application journey.

In fact, EssaySnark has for years asked all of our clients to do what we call a "Career Goal Statement" as the very first step of our consulting engagement. You would benefit from going through this process, too.

Side note: This is the core of the Career Goals App Accelerator that we offer, which also provides detailed, personalized and private feedback from EssaySnark on the goals you come up with – *before* you start writing your essays.

Columbia's Short-Answer Question: Short-Term Goal

Let's review what Columbia is asking:

> *What is your immediate post-MBA professional goal?* (Maximum of 75 characters.)

This of course is from the Columbia website:

http://www4.gsb.columbia.edu/mba/admissions/applynow/apprequirements

You noticed, of course, did you not, Brave Supplicant, that it says *characters*. Not "words." This is truly a *short* short answer. And in fact, this year it's even shorter. They allowed 200 characters for this in the first two years they asked the question, and then last year cut it down to 100 characters. With this further cut, they're really trying to get you to focus in.

What can we interpret from the fact that they cut the allotted space in half last year, and then by another 25% now?

That you must be CONCISE with what you say.

Okay, great, glad we got that clarified for you.

Oh and by the way, yes, spaces count as characters. The online application allows only a max of that many, it will cut you off if you try to go to 76.

Super short, super sweet.

So do you want to know the other reason that EssaySnark believes is behind this change?

They're trying to signal that the short-answer response you provide is not the full extent of what you need to say about your goals. This answer is important but it's not all that you will be discussing of your plans for your post-MBA life. That needs to be fully fleshed out in the first essay, too. This answer isn't even going to be a full sentence! It's a fragment. That's a clear indication that the full explanation of your "immediate post-MBA goal" needs to go in the essay. This is just a quick shorthand to help you focus, and to easily communicate the essence of why you want the MBA to the adcom.

You'll need to study the examples they've provided – and we're also including here the examples that they provided previously, when they allowed for more words in this answer.

To underscore this need for brevity and straightforwardedness that Columbia is broadcasting loud and clear with the 75-character limit, let's compare the examples they used to give with those they are offering now:

> *Old Example (200-character limit):*
>
> "After my MBA I want to build my expertise in the energy sector and learn more about strategy and decision making by joining a consulting firm specializing in renewable energy and power companies."
>
> *Current Example (100-character limit):*
>
> "After my MBA I want to join a consulting firm specializing in renewable energy and power companies."
>
> *Old Example (200-character limit):*
>
> "After my MBA I hope to work in business development for a media company that is expanding its market share in Asia."
>
> "I hope to work in business development for a media company that is expanding its reach in Asia."
>
> *Old Example (200-character limit):*
>
> "My short term goal is to work with an investment firm that utilizes public private partnerships to invest in community development projects."
>
> *Old Example (100-character limit):*
>
> "My goal is to work for an investment firm that focuses on community development projects."
>
> *New Examples (75-character limit):*
>
> "Work in business development for a media company."
> "Join a consulting firm specializing in renewable energy."
> "Work for an investment firm that focuses on real estate."

We pity the poor Brave Supplicant who *really wants to do one of these three examples* because Columbia is going to be a little suspicious if your short answer sounds just like them. We do appreciate that they offered some examples, however they've also potentially done a disservice to any applicant who was really truly wanting to target a career in one of these areas. And, we're also certain that some Brave Supplicants will simply copy-and-paste, or copy-and-tweak, these examples into their CBS apps. Not advised, dear Supplicant.

Next, we call attention to the fact that this is what Columbia has ALWAYS asked its applicants — they're just now really forcing people to be explicit and clear. For years and years, Columbia had an unchanging "essay 1" that used to read:

> What are your short-term and long-term post-MBA goals? How will Columbia Business School help you achieve these goals? *[OLD VERSION]*

Both this short-answer question, and the current incarnation of their essay 1, are really asking the same thing as that Columbia classic. The big difference is, Columbia used to allow 750 words to cover that; now you get 500 words ... and 75 characters.

One advantage to tackling the Columbia app first is that, as we mentioned earlier, the work you'll do on this short-answer response will help you tremendously in being clear and direct when you answer other schools' career goals essays. For a couple years, Wharton had a super-short essay on goals – a recent version of their question was this:

> How will the Wharton MBA help you achieve your professional objectives? (400 words) *[OLD VERSION]*

That's a short essay but believe it or not, when Wharton introduced this question in 2011, they only allowed 300 words with it! That's just one paragraph, basically. If you've not started writing any essays yet, you may not have an appreciation for how tough these limits are.

None of this is too relevant to this discussion of how to answer Columbia's essays, except to point out that what works at Columbia often works at Wharton — they tend to focus on similar elements of candidate's profiles in their admissions process.

Snarky Strategy #4

If you nail these career goals down for Columbia, *you might be in good shape to apply to Wharton, too.*[1]

Again, do the Columbia app first. Go through these exercises and spend time refining your answers. Then, after you've got your pitch solid, turn to your next app. If you want that to be Wharton, cool, you'll be set up for some success with at least a few of the building blocks in hand. (Just remember, you can't apply to Wharton in Round 1 and Columbia in Early Decision unless you're willing to walk away from the Wharton application – yes, even if they admit you. With an ED app, you are agreeing in advance to attend Columbia.)

---

1 Provided your profile is strong, obviously

So how do you get your career goals in good shape for Columbia, and Wharton, and all these other great schools?

Well, since we really truly want to be helpful to you, because you plunked down your hard-earned cash for this here guide, we're going to lay out an exercise which we've used with our full-service consulting clients for years. This is more than just to address the short-answer question. This exercise will inform your entire strategy to every school (except for MIT, who don't even ask about the goals, and Harvard which is also not obsessed about them, though they're not completely irrelevant there either).

EssaySnark's career goals exercise for new clients

Please complete this fill-in-the-blank exercise. This is a good first step for you to develop career goals, in order to demonstrate to the adcom what you want to do and why an MBA is essential:

1. "After I get my MBA I will be/do X" [add as much detail as you can - job title, industry or niche, functional area, specialty, example companies to work for, geography, etc.].

[Write your answer here. Go ahead. Nobody will look at it.]

_____

_____

_____

_____

2. "My long term goal is to do Y" [less detail needed but must be clear and specific, and rational, given the s/t goal]

[Write this one down, too.]

_____

_____

_____

_____

3. "An MBA from Columbia is critical for me to achieve this because:" [solid reasons that point to the differentiation offered by Columbia are critical here — you'll want to express how it will explicitly give you the skills you need for the short-term goal]

[This bit is important. Use more space if you need to.]

_____

_____

_____

> **4. "Now is the right time for me to get an MBA because:"** [a younger candidate would include a quick statement of why they feel they're ready; other candidates might describe how they need the MBA to take advantage of the opportunities they see in their industry; all candidates should be able to articulate a handful of examples for why they're poised and ready to make this next jump in career. This can be answered in a lot of different ways. You need to come up with multiple reasons for "why MBA?" and "why now?".]
>
> *[This year, Columbia is explicit about wanting an answer to this.]*
>
> _____
>
> _____
>
> _____
>
> The short-term goal should have significant detail, and the bschool experience needs to be the setup for that (bschool should be positioned as the best means possible to prepare you for that short-term goal).
>
> The long-term goal needs much less detail but it needs to be logical and achievable, given the interim goals. You wouldn't want to position bschool as prep for the long-term goal, only for the short-term one.

Yes, even though Columbia isn't asking for a "title" in their essay question, it wouldn't hurt to put one in. The specificity can take you far. It shows that you've put some thought into it, that you've researched the options, that you know the industry. That level of detail truly cannot hurt you.

So what's a bad career goal?

Columbia offered some good examples of "professional goals". Let's look at a few more.

"I want to become a leader in the financial services industry."

We see this all the time. Sorry folks. "Leader" is meaningless. And, believe it or not, so is "financial services." Much too broad. Are you talking about a big bank? A hedge fund? A mutual fund or other investment management company? Even insurance companies are often lumped into "financial services." This sentence is near-meaningless. It doesn't tell us anything about *what you want to do*.

Here's another one:

"I want to be on the executive team of a multinational corporation."

Same problem. Sure, "executive team" has a little more specificity than "leader" however it still doesn't tell us *what you want to do*. (Note the theme?) And "multinational corporation" is just a blob of a term. What type of corporation? In which country? If you're interested in some type of international angle to your career, then you need to say that! This phrase is communicating next to nothing — except to say that maybe you haven't really put that much thought into it yet.

The other issue with both of these is timing. It's unrealistic to assume you'll be much of a "leader" — at least, not on a grand scale of anything — within the timeframe that Columbia is asking you to present with these career goals. Nobody can see the future. Nobody knows what you'll be doing in 15 years. And that's how long it takes for most people to gain the experience, skills, and connections to actually become a CFO or what have you. It's highly unlikely you'll be rocking that boat within the timeframe expected in a "short/long-term goals" question from any school.

Instead, you need to focus on literally what type of job you'll get right when you come out of Columbia. That's what they mean by the word "immediate" in the question, right? They added that qualifier after the first year of using this question, since they clearly didn't get answers that were targeted enough.

For the purposes of this exercise we've laid out, you need to define that "immediate" job, and then carve out a plan for how you'll progress from there, to perhaps another position, and at most, one more, which you'll identify as your long-term target. Even though Columbia essay 1 doesn't use the phrase "long-term goal", it's what you should be discussing there — that, and why you want to go to their school. So don't skip that part of this exercise.

Most people are promoted maybe once every two years. If you consider that your long-term goal should be in the 5- to 8-year post-MBA timeframe, that will help you see (hopefully) what might be a realistic target to present for the adcom. **Given where you're at today in your career (level/role/ title/ responsibilities), what is a probable trajectory for you to end up in, say, the year 2025?**

Yeah, we know. That feels like forever away. But map it out for yourself and see where you end up. Envision your future. Project your life away onto the horizon of time and find out where it goes.

Here's even a little bit of space for you to capture your thinking on this. Yes, right here. Go ahead.

_____

_____

_____

_____

_____

_____

We just told you that you can't say you want to be "on the executive team" - that it's too ambiguous of a goal, and it's also too ambitious. There is one exception to this, where it might fly to tell the adcom that you'll be "CEO", and that is this: If you're going to be working in a family business after you graduate. If that's the case, then it's fine to say you're going to be taking over the whole show. You have different challenges than most people in presenting your goals (it's outside the scope of this *Guide* to discuss them but we can coach you on them if you sign up for our services). However, when constructed in the right way, this "CEO" goal could work fine in being realistic and achievable for a certain type of candidate.

But we've gotten ahead of ourselves. All this goes in Essay 1. We were still looking at the short-answer question. Let's go back. Let's talk about that "realistic and achievable" thing we just mentioned.

It's so important that we're making it Snarky Strategy #5

Your career goals must be both *realistic* and *achievable*.

OK, we've said it now three times in three paragraphs. And we alluded to it already, with the comments about timeframe and what's feasible to accomplish in the long-term goal horizon that the school expects. The Columbia adcom is really, truly, going to look at your goals and see if they make sense. Are they believable? Is this a plan that you will be able to pull off? Is it do-able? Or is what you're saying more like a pipe dream? A fancy idea? A fantasy?

The important takeaway message here is: *don't make stuff up.* The point of this exercise is not to present the most amazing, aggressive, flamboyant-sounding goals the school has ever seen. Actually, it's usually much more effective to present goals that are very standard, traditional, perhaps even run-of-the-mill.

Bschool candidates are always told that they have to stand out, that they have to differentiate themselves. Well guess what? **The career goals is not the place to do this.**

- **People are admitted to Columbia because they have clear, rational, logical goals that Columbia knows they can help them achieve.**
- **People are admitted to Columbia because the Columbia MBA is obviously going to be an accelerator for them to achieve success in their lives, to go out and contribute to the world (and, hopefully, to contribute to Columbia as an alumni later on).**

The best way to impress the Columbia adcom is to show them that you've already worked hard and built your education/career up to a certain point, and that you have a plan for where you want to take it from here, and you're looking for the advantage of a Columbia MBA to do so.

This means, you want to present career goals that MAKE SENSE, both given who YOU are, and given what COLUMBIA is.

This is the essence of "school fit" – a term that gets bandied about in bschool admissions circles and which many people have no clue about.

- If you're looking to use bschool to make some **radical career change**, you have a bigger challenge. You need to show the adcom that you have transferable skills and are equipped to make the transition to the new field. This can be especially critical for those going in a dissimilar direction, e.g., IT guys wanting to go into finance. You'll need to show how you're ready to make this leap.
- Conversely, if you're not showing ENOUGH transition — if your stated **short-term goal is too similar** (or even identical) to what you are already currently doing in your job today — then you're not giving the adcom enough evidence of why you need an MBA. You should position yourself as ADVANCING, and then show how the MBA is the one main requirement that you need to get from A to B.

A Snarky Caveat

The three most common mistakes with Columbia career goals are:

* They're too vague

* They're too ambitious

* They're too broad

If your goals suffer from any of these sins, it's highly unlikely Columbia will let you in. Too vague means terminology like "financial services" or "executive team." Too ambitious is a goal that's written to impress the reader instead of being attainable for the candidate's actual skills and experience. Too broad is often when the applicant can't make up his mind and so he brings in multiple options of "I could do this or I might do that."

While it could very well be true that you will pursue different options and paths once you're in the process of earning your MBA, it is usually a mistake to try and present all these different options to the Columbia adcom in their essays. There simply isn't room to provide an appropriate level of detail on more than one possible career path. The Columbia adcom tends to reward candidates who express confidence and conviction, who sound like they have an honest-to-goodness action plan. Sure, your life may take you in a different direction once the wheels are in motion. What the Columbia folks want to see is that you're mature and responsible, that you know how to take control of your life and that you're able to make your own success. A well-crafted set of Columbia essays will communicate this implicitly (no, we do not recommend that you literally tell the adcom that you have done that or are that type of person).

In a nutshell: Keeping that *realistic and achievable* guideline in mind as you refine your goals should help you avoid these problems.

Also note: Columbia does not typically admit career-changers to the J-Term. Why not? Because the standard two-year full-time MBA experience has been designed around the internship. The summer internship is where you gain experience, network, and, these days, often a permanent job offer. If you're switching gears to do something different after you graduate, the internship is critical. The J-Term by definition is an accelerated program with no internship.

Thus, the Columbia adcom is highly unlikely to buy a pitch saying you'll do a major about-face in your career without an internship. So don't even try that, it's not going to work.

By now, you're wondering, "EssaySnark, are we talking about that 'immediate post-MBA professional goal' short answer? Or are we in Essay 1 territory now?"

And you're right, the lines have blurred a bit, have they not? Let's move on.

Columbia's Essay 1: Why MBA (Which Is Really: Goals)

Columbia asks:

> *Given your individual background and goals, why are you pursuing a Columbia MBA at this time?* (Maximum of 500 words.)

What they asked several years ago:

> *Considering your post-MBA and long term professional goals, why are you pursuing an MBA at this point in your career? Additionally, why is Columbia Business School a good fit for you?* (Maximum of 750 words.)

From the Columbia website at:

http://www8.gsb.columbia.edu/programs-admissions/mba/admissions/application-requirements#5

Why do we keep talking about what Columbia used to ask in these essays?

To show you the constant emphasis on goals.

Despite the fact that their questions have changed from year to year, they're really looking for the same stuff in a candidate. And, to emphasize how much they want you to be succinct. They used to allow a lot more space to go over your future plans. But candidates just blathered on and didn't say what they should've been saying. So Columbia cut the limit down, to force you to think more carefully about your answer.

This is why the exercises we've provided here are so useful, and it's also why we recommend that you develop outlines before you start writing a single word of an actual essay draft. (We have an Essay Ideas App Accelerator that walks you through the process of developing outlines for all the essays for a single school.)

What needs to go in Essay 1?

Or, *how to do it.*

First, this essay needs a balance of THE FUTURE and THE PAST. You may think that they're not asking anything about the past here. If you think that, you're mistaken. The first part of the sentence - "Given your individual background" – that is a direct request that you give some reasons for why you're qualified for the goals you're going to espouse for yourself.

This needs to be treated carefully. You should highlight one or two key examples that set you up as qualified – briefly. In a way that adds to their understanding of your background.

Remember, they can read your resume if they need to know the entirety of your professional history. What you want to focus on instead is identifying something concrete and specific that encapsulates your awesomeness and how you're prepared for the challenges of the future job you've identified with the short-answer response. It's definitely relevant to include a quick recap of who you are/what you've done, to set context – all of this from a professional standpoint. Just do not go overboard. There should be no more than a portion of one paragraph of background info. We like to see this in the first paragraph, but it could go anywhere in the essay – it just needs to be *somewhere* in the essay.

Also, recognize that they've used the phrase "individual background." What they mean by that is, what makes you unique? How are you differentiated? And in the context of "background and goals", how is your past experience perfectly suited to help you pursue the goals you're stating?

The example(s) from your past you use in this part of your essay will be a critical component of your pitch. It needs to show, not just how you're qualified for your short-term career goal, but how you're qualified for admission to Columbia business school.

And also note that your "individual background" is NOT the same as your "personal life." We strongly (STRONGLY) recommend that you focus exclusively on career/professional/work experiences in this essay. There are some exceptions to this but they are few and far between. For almost everyone, Columbia Essay 1 should have no personal anecdotes or stories; it needs to be career-focused only.

Along those lines: The thing they've asked at end of the essay prompt is important. You may have overlooked that little qualifier "at this time." What they're doing with that is they're saying, "please focus on WHO YOU ARE TODAY." You need to be demonstrating your readiness for bschool, today, now – and this comes through best when you limit your material in this essay to things you've done most recently. We recommend sticking to stories from the past three years. Unless you're coming straight from university, avoid talking about college experiences; they're probably not too relevant to who you are today. The adcom wants to know what you've done since you've graduated.

Again, there may be exceptions to this past-three-years rule, but they will be rare. If you're tempted to dive deeper into your past for the examples that you want to include in this, we invite you to reconsider. We almost always push back on BSers who present stories in such an essay that are older than that. We almost definitely would push back on you if you were to do so. These exceptions are unusual. It is unlikely that you are one of them. Sure, maybe you are – but unlikely. Think carefully before giving yourself the green-light to include stories that are not within the last three years in Columbia Essay 1.

This element of Columbia Essay 1 is how you express "school fit" – that is, how are you a fit to the school. You do this by showing them, with something definite and specific, how you've been a strong achiever in your career to date. You do this by describing – in as few words as humanly possible – one or two examples from your life when you've done something great. Important stuff, this. This is how you elevate your essay from the pack. This is where the rubber meets the road in terms of standing out from the crowd. Yeah, it's hard. And really, really important.

Finally: What do they mean when they say "why are you pursuing a Columbia MBA?" You'd think this was the easy part – after all, it's the crux of the question, right? Everybody should be able to deal with that.

Ha. We wish. You'd be surprised how many essays we read where people come off completely far from the mark. People often spew out complete drafts of MBA application essays that go *blah blah blah* and provide no answer to the question. There will be many people who do that with this question, too. Don't you be one of them.

The "why MBA?" thing is pretty straightforward. But in case you are unclear, we're going to break it down:

They want you to explain why you want an MBA.

You have to have a better reason than just, "Because I want one."

And not just why you need any old MBA. They want to hear about why you want to get a *Columbia* MBA.

That means, look at your career goals – the immediate post-MBA one that you're stating in your short-answer response, and the longer-term one that you carved out in the exercise you did previously. Now look at the "how I'm qualified" stuff that should have been encapsulated in what you worked out in Part 4 of that career goals exercise that we gave you (turn back to page 19 if you need a reminder). Now look at the deltas between the two.

You want to go *there*. You're starting *here*. What do you need in order for you to go from this starting place to that destination? Theoretically, that should all be stuff that a Columbia MBA can give you. And so theoretically, that should form the core of this essay.

The other very important angle is not just the technicalities of why you need an MBA, but why you want to go to Columbia. What's unique about Columbia that's attracted you to apply there? What do you feel you can get there that maybe you wouldn't be able to get anywhere else? This is where you express "school fit" – how the school is a fit to you.

You'll want to be exceptionally detailed and specific here (while still being concise, of course).

This is where all that on-the-ground research that you've been conducting for the past few months will pay off. This is where you get to tell the adcom that you visited a class (tell them when, and which one) and you talked to a student (tell them who) and you learned such-and-such about what Columbia offers, and this is why that's important to you.

A straightforward structure for CBS 1 is — and this is just an example, your essay need not conform to this exactly:

- **INTRO/PARA 1 (1/3 of the essay): We think it's a nice technique to open with a restatement of the goal you identified in your short-answer response. It's better to rephrase that sentence somehow; don't repeat it verbatim. Alternatively, you could directly answer the essay question here: "I'm pursuing an MBA from Columbia because..." That's a little clunky, it can feel abrupt to start that way, but it could work. A more sophisticated approach is to layer in something specific about you and your background or qualifications and weave that** into your opening. Maybe something like:

"Based on my three years in private equity, I am now ready to go to business school so that I can pursue the next challenge of moving into venture capital." You can also state your longer-term goal somewhere in the opening, too, or you can circle back to that later.

- **Then, move into your examples. Briefly recap** what you've done in your career, with specifics. Tell a story or give an example if possible. To illustrate: "Since joining ABC Partners as an Analyst in 2011, I have built strong skills in this and that through my success leading such-and-such projects." Even this is nowhere near as detailed as your examples need to be, but we're providing a model so you can get a sense of what we mean. Even though this is not enough, there's still something to hang onto: the reader has been told the company name, the job title, how long on the job, and it's even got some statements of achievement that start to express the applicant's competencies. In your "brief recap" paragraph you could possibly go all the way back to college and quickly explain why you chose the major that you did, or you could explain any sideways turns in your career (e.g., "Even though I studied film at UCLA, I took a job in commercial real estate when I graduated because..."), or you could tell a story of how you became inspired to pursue your new career goals. This first paragraph should give the reader a little context. This is where you can answer the "individual background" angle. Or, you could cover this later on — or possibly not at all, depending on your approach to this essay.

- **PARA 2 (1/3 of essay): Goals** Here you should flesh out what you stated in the short answer. You need to give the details around that "professional goal" in order to give it life. Define/explain/express/illustrate what you want to do when you graduate from Columbia. Remember that "hireability" thing we mentioned before; this is where the adcom can test that you've got a plan for your own success. You can also include some references to your long-term goal. However, since Columbia has not explicitly asked for a long-term goal, it is NOT necessary to include one. If you do include it, it must be rational and logical, given the immediate post-MBA goal you've specified, and you need to give at least a little bit of context or detail around it. You can't just toss out something at random and leave it at that. Better to skip the long-term goal entirely than do a drive-by with it. (We do recommend including it if you can, but we know that many people will go through convulsions over the limited space available, and this is technically optional since the adcom has not asked for it.)

- **PARA 3 (1/3 of essay):** Why MBA/why Columbia? The focus should be on the latter question, which implicitly answers the former. Why have you chosen CBS, over the gazillion other great schools out there, to achieve these stated goals? This is where you seed in specifics like classes, faculty, clubs, programs, resources, etc. Tell them that you visited campus on [date] and got all inspired by [such and such]. Show them how much homework you've done But, make it relevant. Link in these school-specific references to your exact needs. Do a gap analysis — see where you're lacking and how the CBS education can fill those gaps, then identify the resources that will do it. This can be hard skills, soft skills, or both. Make all this tailored to Columbia. And, keep in mind that you're getting the opportunity to cover Columbia-specific material in essay 2. Be sure these two pieces work well together.

- **CONCLUSION**: Wrap up with a recap statement of why you want an MBA from Columbia, ideally restating your career goals and/or referencing something specific about the program, etc. Can be just a sentence. Don't skip this, else the essay will feel unfinished.

So there you go: a map to Columbia Essay 1. Remember that these are all just ideas. Obviously you'll need to make your essay your own. We shouldn't have to say this but we will: Please be very careful about copying anything we suggest verbatim. We sell a lot of these essay guides, and we know some adcoms make a habit of buying them. It would be a real shame for our words to end up in your essay – particularly since the schools use plagiarism checking software.

Essay 2: Columbia at the Center

Last year Columbia asked what we thought was a silly question:

> *Columbia Business School is located in the heart of the world's business capital - Manhattan. How do you anticipate that New York City will impact your experience at Columbia?* [OLD VERSION]

We did a whole rant on the EssaySnark blahg about the fact that Columbia is NOT in the "heart" of New York City. They're just not. So we were very pleased to see them abandon that idea in this year's question – though we're certain it wasn't due to our complaints about it. The problem with last year's question was that everyone ended up writing the same gosh darn thing in their Columbia essay 2. Over and over again, we read about how people were going to do like three main things based on Columbia's NYC location – and all those things were what Columbia admissions was chatting up in every info session. Boooorrrrrrr-rrrrrinnnnnng. We're certain that last year's essay 2s were pretty repetitive and didn't reveal much for the adcom.

This year's version is better:

> *[Watch video on their site, then answer the question]* How will you take advantage of being "at the very center of business"?

Not only does this question incorporate Columbia's new messaging and tagline about "CBS at the Center" (if that phrase is new to you then you obvious haven't been on their website or Twitter feed enough) – but this new essay 2 prompt is also much more open-ended.

We do believe that many people will end up going down the same paths as others do with this question, but we strongly encourage you to reflect on what "at the center of business" means – not just as a geographic advantage, which NYC certainly could be for your career. There's other directions you could go with this. Why not do some brainstorming or spend five minutes of word association, free thinking about this phrase? That would be a great place to begin with your ideas.

In fact, one suggestion would be to do that autonomous brainstorming FIRST – before you watched the video (though you probably already did that). Then you could compare your ideas to what Columbia feels is important with this 'center of business" concept. Creating a little Venn diagram of the intersection of those ideas is where you will find your best ideas for this essay.

Remember, this essay needs to be about how you'll maximize your opportunities at Columbia. It should be about you, and about Columbia. Beware the risk of going off on tangents. This is probably not the essay to talk about how you were so excited to visit the Statue of Liberty when you were ten years old and you've always wanted to come back to New York. Stay focused on your goals – which are always *your career goals* and communicating to the adcom how Columbia Business School will help you achieve them.

What needs to go in Essay 2?

Your job with this essay is not to list out all the great things about New York. If you decide to talk about the geography, then you should be clear on your *reasons why those great New York things matter to you.*

The best essays for this question take a very individualized approach. They don't just rattle off a bunch of features of Columbia or of Manhattan. They talk about why those things are important to the Brave Supplicant, and what the Brave Supplicant is going to do with them.

So as we just stated: You need to make this essay about YOU. Not about New York.

You can use this essay in conjunction with Essay 1 to answer more of "why I want to go to Columbia Business School." In fact, you *should* do that. If you find that you just don't have enough space in Essay 1 to cover all the things you want to – scratch that. *When* you find that you don't have enough space in Essay 1, you can look to Essay 2 as a possible place to sneak in some of them.

This, again, is why it's so helpful to do outlines before start writing. If you sketch out what's going to go in each essay, before you start writing any of them, then you have this great opportunity to do some slicing and dicing, and juggling, and rearranging around of your material. You can finagle your needful things in different ways, and better optimize your messaging among the separate questions that they've asked you.

Essay 2, we predict, will be pretty fun to write. Most people want to go to Columbia not just because it's Columbia, an Ivy League *ooooh*-inducing institution, but just as much because it's in New York. The key strategy is that you must make sure you share something new ABOUT YOURSELF in this essay. You can't just write how much you love the Big Apple. You need to impart some wisdom about you as well.

Use the invitation of this second essay to really explore Columbia. Put some time into thinking about how you'd leverage your experience there. The net result of this effort is that you'll be a much more educated consumer of what Columbia can offer to you — and, hopefully, you'll be a much better informed applicant who can show reasons why Columbia is the right place for you to get your MBA.

This essay can include some personal stuff if you like; it doesn't have to be solely professional, though the bulk of it should be. Obviously, 250 words is *short*. Real short. You will need to write and rewrite and edit this one. You don't need an extensive, drawn-out introduction and conclusion – but you should have a smooth opening, and a wrap-up sentence, so that it feels polished. Don't just barf up a bunch of stuff at the reader. Give it a real beginning and ending and it'll be more satisfying to read.

And don't forget to watch the video. You don't want to cue your entire answer off of that, but it would be nice if, when reading your essay, the adcom could tell that you had seen the video and were writing about something that's somehow relevant. (You might also want to watch the videos they used in last year's question, which are linked from the Columbia Essay Questions page on the EssaySnark site; those videos include snippets of actual students talking about their experiences.)

Please do not parrot what the voiceover in the video says though! Put your own spin on it. Give the adcom your take of the advantages of NYC and Columbia. Again, as we've said, this needs to be personal, with some type of insight about you offered up. No carbon-copy essays, please.

Columbia's Essay 3: Who Are You?

> *What will the people in your Cluster be pleasantly surprised to learn about you?* (250 words.)

Another shorty. These 250-word essays will likely prove very challenging to you.

This one should also be fun to write. Many schools have had essays like this in recent years, and we expect several other schools to be asking something similar again this year (at the time of this writing, Columbia was the only one with essay questions out). Here's your chance to reveal something authentic and unusual.

What needs to go in Essay 3?

Something honest. Something direct. Something that's just one thing.

It's tempting to turn this into a laundry list of all the things that are unique about you. That's not what the adcom has asked for. However, we often get these kitchen-sink essays from people, where they feel compelled to tell the reader everything they can possibly fit into the tight 250-word space. This essay is not asking for your autobiography. It's also not asking for multiple examples. It's asking for one specific item about you, from your life, that's "surprising."

One way to go with this is to identify an important event that happened in your life, something distinct, and write up the story of what happened. The trick is, you need to be at the center of the story. This only works if the story somehow encapsulates who you are — in a way that is relevant to the adcom. And it must pass the test of "surprising."

Remember also the defining word: "pleasantly." You should NOT use this essay to tell the adcom about how your sister committed suicide. While someone would likely be very shocked to hear about it – and while we're certainly sorry if anything that hugely tragic has happened to you – such a story just doesn't belong in this bschool essay. This essay should be positive, even upbeat if possible.

And this essay needs to be personal. You're already covering your professional self in the short-answer response, in Essay 1, and in (at least most of, if not all of) Essay 2. This one should be something from who you really are as a person, outside of work.

It's not required, but this essay might work best if you keep the focus on something that happened recently, like within the last five years or so. We're very flexible on this recommendation; there's plenty of topics that could qualify for a good Columbia Essay 3 that happened when the applicant was very young. But when thinking about what to share, we do think you should start with stuff that's in the recent past.

Often the greatest essays for topics like this come from the very first thing that popped into your head when you read the question for the first time. If you had a brilliant light-bulb moment like that, then you may want to trust your instincts and go with it.

If you didn't have a big "Aha!" moment the instant you read the essay question, that's OK – you can still end up with a great essay! We recommend doing some brainstorming around what might be a good answer. Make some lists. Think about who you are and what interesting things you've done or experienced.

However, you must resist the urge at all costs to try to think about something that you think sounds impressive. The point of this essay is NOT to say what you think they want you to say. Believe the 'Snark, this is not an essay to talk about how you do volunteer work with kids, or how you ran a marathon. *Maybe* you could fit a quick reference to one of those things in here, but usually that approach makes for one big fat yawn as your reaction from your reader.

That "pleasantly surprised" part means that you need to run your answer through that angle as the test. Is this thing you're going to write about something that a complete stranger, who knows you only through having read your other essays, would have the "pleasantly surprised" reaction to, when they heard about it after reading through the rest of your other essays.

This essay needs to be solely focused on who you are as individual. You *might* be able to talk about how you are engaged with your community in terms of volunteer work, or how you were captain of the football team in college, or some other such thing... but those things are very common. How "surprising" would a stranger be, really, if you shared those facts?

You may want to challenge yourself to dig deeper on this one.

A Snarky Caveat

There is definitely such a thing as TMI here!

In evaluating whether your idea is essay-worthy, ask whether you would tell it to a prospective employer in an interview. If not, it probably doesn't belong in a bschool essay. Remember, this is an application to a professional program. It's less of a risk that BSers will be treading into TMI territory with this essay, than they did in previous years when Columbia asked everyone to share about a "life experience" - but still, it could happen in the current version of the question. Be very conscious about the context, that this is a formal application to BUSINESS school. Even though there will be many, many Happy Hours to attend when you're a future student at Columbia, it's probably not the greatest strategy to write about how you're the reigning champion Jell-O Shots Shooter at your sorority, and that you like the cherry Jell-O the best.

Surprising to the adcom reader, yes indeed, that would be. Pleasantly so? Maybe, in terms of humor quotient. Appropriate for what this is you're writing for? Probably not.

A big warning on Columbia Essay 3: The cliché subject for this essay is travel. You would be surprised how many bschool applicants have been to 10+ different countries (or have run a marathon; that's the other subject that comes up over and over in essays). If you can pull out one specific thing from an experience like that, and zoom in on it in how you explain it to the reader, and importantly, demonstrate why it's unique, so that it's crystal clear how it would be "surprising", then sure, a topic like that can work. But it's way more difficult.

If you traveled somewhere truly exotic, then that may qualify, but you shouldn't just say that you went to Antarctica; you'd want to describe how the experience changed you, and also tell why you went, and when, and maybe what it was like... These are all angles that you could cover – again, just suggestions.

Our simple advice on this one is, don't worry about trying to say the write "bschool essay" thing. Instead, think about it as if you were on a blind date, and the person just walked into the restaurant where you were meeting them, and they were way more attractive than you expected. When you're making conversation with this person, getting to know them for the first time, what would you share with them? What would you say to become friends? Not stuff that you want to impress them with, but stuff that makes them know who you are. What would you want them to know about you?

Something in that category would make a fine answer to Columbia Essay 3.

Optional Essay

This advice is true for any school, not just Columbia: If you don't have something specific that is a) important; and b) that you just cannot for the life of you figure out how to cover appropriately in the main essays... then you should write the optional essay.

For any school, your strategy should be to not overstay your welcome. Like a polite and respectful guest, you should enter the Columbia admissions team's domain, offering exactly what they have asked for in their essay prompts and application instructions, and then exit gracefully.

FOR EXAMPLE...

If you have a gap in your career history, that would be a valid subject to explain in an optional essay. HOWEVER, an astute and creative applicant might find a way to explain it in Essay 1.

Another relevant subject to cover in the optional essay would be a low GPA, provided that you actually have real information to provide to help the adcom understand what was going on with you during your undergraduate experience. Appropriate essays on grades might cover items such as working your way through college, or an extreme personal situation like the illness of a family member. That sort of thing. You probably will not gain points for honesty by just saying that you were didn't take school seriously and were partying too much. (Keep in mind that Columbia puts an emphasis on grades, and so if you're going to call attention to a low GPA, then you'd better have some good reasons to offer AND you hopefully also can tell them about some class you've taken recently where you pulled an A and impressed the professor.) We cover the perennial question of "what to do about a low GPA" on our blahg.

Columbia used to require that an optional essay be written in the case where you're not providing them with a letter of recommendation from your current supervisor. If you don't want to alert your boss that you might be leaving soon to go back to school, that's perfectly fine and legit. Now, instead of covering this in a separate essay, Columbia has added a field to the online application to tell them about it. You should simply explain the situation (briefly!) in the field, telling the adcom why you chose the recommenders that you did instead of your supervisor. Ideally, in such a case, at least one of your recommenders will be a supervisor from a previous job.

If you have multiple issues to explain, you should include them all in a single optional essay. Your final length for this one should not go past 500 words, and much, much shorter is infinitely better.

Remember: Do not outstay your welcome! You may think that writing essays is hard, but EssaySnark can tell you, reading them for days on end is absolutely exhausting. Do not submit more to the adcom than they truly need in order to understand who you are and what you're about.

Reapplicant Essay

This *SnarkStrategies Guide* is not designed to provide all the advice and guidance that a reapplicant to Columbia Business School would need. Instead, you should pick up *The Reapplicant's Guide*, where we lay out everything that you need to turn your situation into a success.

Suffice it to say, if you're reapplying, you should most definitely do so in the Early Decision round. The challenge, of course, is that you'll submit just one new essay, and the question they want you to answer is focusing on how you've improved your profile since your original application.

The disheartening fact is that many Brave Supplicants are misguided in their quest for a Columbia MBA and they think that, since the final deadline is in April each year, that this means they have plenty of time and can submit an application that late and still have a real go at it. As we've been discussing, such is not the case. So what happens is, they apply really late in the season (February or later is considered "late" at this school), and they're not accepted, and then they want to go at it again when the next application opens up – but it's only been a few short months since their original application. And the way to get into Columbia as a reapplicant is to have something significant to point to in terms of how you've improved your profile.

The most obvious ways are to increase the GMAT (if that was a weakness – if it was already over, say, 700 total, then this may not be a workable strategy) and take a class (if the college GPA is a little low). Or, if you get a shiny new promotion or move into a completely new role at work, then that's definitely worth reporting and can often be seen as significant enough for the adcom to admit.

Columbia is friendly to reapplicants. They just need to see proof that you're now ready for bschool. It is not enough to simply write better essays with clearer sentences and no typos. You need to actually show them why you're a better candidate today than you were the first time around.

If you have specific questions on how to tackle a reapplication to Columbia Business School, be sure to stop by the blahg or drop us an email and we'll see what we can do to help.

What to Do Next

This is not meant as an end-all, be-all guide on all things Columbia. In fact, if you REALLY want to go to this school, you'd do yourself a favor by going to NYC and actually visit the place. Hang out on the UWS. See what the campus is like. Explore the unfortunately named Uris Hall. Sit in on a class. Ask questions. Meet people.

No, Columbia won't deny your app just because you didn't visit campus, but truly, it can make a big difference in knowing what the school is about and knowing whether it's the right place for you (plus it'll give you additional ammo to put into your essays).

Also, remember that the way Columbia admissions process goes means you can be in for a stressful few months as you experience the waiting game after you submit. Resist the temptation to try and overinterpret every little nuance of the process. You might get invited to interview really quickly – or it may take ages. You might get an answer back after the interview – or you may end up waiting around for many weeks. In general, yes, they tend to act more quickly on the strongest applications, but just because you're in a holding pattern does not mean you're doomed!

In no cases does EssaySnark ever recommend that you contact the admissions office to find out about your decision. You just have to be patient. If you are pushy or seem to not be able to follow directions, you could jeopardize your chances! After you've put together the strongest application you can, then it's time to let it go and move on with your life. Find some new project to dive into to distract yourself (volunteering is always good!!) and don't worry about it. You've done all you can. Just let it be and see what happens. Soon enough, you'll get the news. There is nothing you can do to accelerate the adcom's timetable. Remember, they are working through huge volumes of other candidates, and they're trying to be fair to everyone. Give them the time and space they need to do their job.

Oh yeah: You should know that Columbia tends to call people when they're admitting them. They tend to make the calls during morning hours Eastern time on business days. (They will know what timezone you're in and it's unlikely they will call you in the middle of the night.) After you interview, keep your cell phone close by, and be sure to pick up if you get a call from an unknown number or blocked line!

We wish you the very best of luck with your Columbia Business School application!

Want more help?

Swing over to the EssaySnark blahg at http://essaysnark.com to ask a question, or drop us an email at gethelpnow@essaysnark.com to inquire about our specialized MBA consulting services for Columbia and all the other top bschools of the world.

One last thing: If you found value in this *Guide*, it would be totally awesome if you would stop back by the website where you bought it – Amazon, or essaysnark.com, or wherever – and leave some feedback about it, to let others know!

We'd be truly grateful.

www.ingramcontent.com/pod-product-compliance
Lightning Source LLC
Chambersburg PA
CBHW080528110426
42742CB00017B/3274